Parenting

Navigating everything

STUDY GUIDE

by Brett Ullman

Printed in Canada

Print ISBN: 978-1-4866-2324-2
eBook ISBN: 978-1-4866-2325-9

This study guide corresponds with *Parenting: Navigating Everything* by Brett Ullman (2020). Available wherever fine Christian books are sold.
Print ISBN: 978-1-4866-1701-2
eBook ISBN: 978-1-4866-1702-9

Word Alive Press
119 De Baets Street, Winnipeg, MB R2J 3R9
www.wordalivepress.ca

Cataloguing in Publication may be obtained through Library and Archives Canada

Study Guide

Welcome to the book study guide for *Parenting: Navigating Everything*. We are inspired by Hebrews 10:24 which says, "let us consider how we may spur one another on toward love and good deeds." Parenting well takes a lot of love and wisdom. We can best learn when we discuss the contents of this book with others. "Building a strong family and raising a strong adult are both cultivated by a purposeful leader who takes the time and makes an effort to turn a vision into a reality through intentional action" (Amy Carney, Parent on Purpose).

This study guide follows the book *Parenting: Navigating Everything* chapter by chapter. This guide will break down the book's content into bite-size pieces and by asking you questions will support you to process and apply what you are learning. Even though you can benefit by going through this guide on your own, we recommend discussing these questions with others in a small group. This can deepen your understanding of how to apply the ideas into your own family. It is also an enjoyable and bonding experience to learn, grow and problem-solve with others.

We suggest discussing one chapter each time you meet. Some chapters have many questions listed, maybe even more than you have time to discuss. We suggest everyone reads the one chapter and answers the questions themselves individually prior to your meeting. Then as a group, you decide what questions you have time to discuss if all of them can't be accommodated.

Thank you for joining in on this most important discussion. We are excited for all you will be learning on this journey. Let's get to it!

Please take some time to answer these questions with your group:

INTRODUCTION:

1 What ages are the children you are currently raising?

2 What is your family composition currently (i.e. who is living in your home?)

3 What are the personality traits of your children?

4 Do any of your children have exceptional needs beyond what is typical for kids their age?

5 Do you have any limitations yourself that affect your parenting? (i.e. health, work schedule, etc.)

6 What has motivated you to participate in this study on parenting?

7 Have you read any parenting books before?

8 What have you heard that has been good parenting advice?

CHAPTER 1: PARENTING

1 What parenting stage are you currently in? Discipline, training, coaching, or friendship? (Page 2)

2 What are you liking about this current stage?

3 Is parenting so far what you expected? Why or why not?

4 What are you finding challenging in this current stage?

5 Are you experiencing anything in parenting currently that you are finding hard to be truthful to others about?

6 How is being a child now different than when you were a child?

7 What do you see as good about children today?

8 What concerns you about children today?

9 How do you see parenting being different now?

10 How do you see parenting being responsible for what is good and bad about children today?

11 What is working well right now in your family?

12 What areas are needing improvement?

13 Do you see any patterns in yourself that contribute to the concerns you are having with your children?

14 What is an issue in society that concerns you the most as you raise your children?

15 What do you see as the goal of your parenting? Have you ever thought that through before? Does it help you to have clarity in your parenting?

16 Why do you think that having your children's happiness as the primary goal could lead to some problems?

CHAPTER 2: PARENTING STYLES

1 What parenting styles best describe you? How about your spouse/their other parent?

2 How do you act as a parent when you are stressed? How about the other parent?

3 What do you like about your parenting style and want to continue?

4 What are some things that would be better to change about your parenting style?

5 What did you find interesting about the other parenting styles?

6 Are there other parenting styles that you sometimes find yourself doing?

7 Which styles are you most wanting to avoid?

8 What are you already doing that promotes your children to be attached to you? How could you add to that to maximize your children's attachment to you?

9 Do you see anything you currently do that would be considered overparenting?

10 How might you change that pattern?

11 Is there something your kids are asking to do that up until now you have said no to?

12 Is there some teaching you could do with them to prepare them for you to say yes?

13 Do both you and their other parent share the responsibility of parenting, or does anything need to change to equalize it?

14 What do you understand about being an "inside-out parent"?

15 Is there anything you need to shift in your thinking to become more inside-out focused?

16 Who is in your "village" speaking into your child's life?

17 Who else is influencing your children currently? Are you content with your present village or do you need to add/change people? If so, who and how?

1 What daily tasks are your children doing for themselves currently?

2 What are you or your spouse/other parent doing for them that you think they could do for themselves now?

3 What 3 skills do you want to prioritize to teach your child/children in the next few weeks?

4 What are the steps you need to take to teach them to be independent with this skill?

5 Do you feel that your parenting is preparing your kids for success in life when you aren't around? If not, what could you change to make that happen?

1   How do you feel about the amount and quality of time you spend with your children?

2   Does the marble analogy change how you view or plan to use your time with your family?

3   How are you managing to fit in the big rocks, little rocks, and sand into your own life?

4   Do you need to prioritize anything differently?

5   How many meals each week are you sharing with your family? Are you satisfied with this number and the quality of the interactions with each family member?

6   What are some things that your family likes to do together?

7   Is there any other activity that you'd like to add?

8   How do you feel about your family's pace of life?

9   Is there anything you'd like to change or cut back on?

10. How do you want your family to look in 10 years?

11. What do you need to do now to start to build toward that vision of your family?

12. How does your family celebrate transitions & milestones, and acknowledge pits?

13. Is there some area you want to start acknowledging with your family?

1. Is there anything about the way you communicate with your child/children that you now see as needing improvement?

2. Have you ever asked your spouse or your child to give you feedback about the way you communicate? Would you be willing to?

3. In what areas do you want to know how you're doing as a parent?

4. Is your relationship with your child/children at the point where they would feel safe to be honest with you?

5   If so, what feedback did you get from your child on your report card? (if they are old enough to complete it)

6   What other questions did you add to the parent report card?

7   How do you plan to address the areas to improve that you discovered?

8   Has your child shared with you something that's hard to hear? How are you showing them that you have heard them?

9   In what areas are you challenged to show unconditional love for your children?

10 What words or lack of words from you are coming to mind that your children would benefit from hearing an apology for?

11 Is there any area of your life that you plan to change knowing that your children are watching and will imitate you? (i.e., driving, talking about other people, your media choices etc.)

12 What are each of your children's love languages?

13 What are your thoughts about having a family meeting? Do you plan on booking a family meeting? Why or why not?

14 If so, what things would you like to have on the family meeting agenda?

1. What's your takeaway from the Bamboo tree story?

2. What are some of your current discipline concerns with your children?

3. How is discipline different than punishment?

4. How do you see daily structure supporting discipline?

5. Are there any structural changes you see as being needed in your family right now?

6   How does modeling support discipline? Are you asking anything of your children that you aren't doing yourself?

7   What are you currently doing to build into your relationship with each one of your children?

8   Do you see any need for improvement in the areas of building up trust and respect between your child and yourself?

9   Is there an area where your expectations need to be spoken out loud to your child?

10 What type of parenting boundaries do you typically demonstrate: stone wall, wild field, or picket fence? If you are not sure, discuss the definitions of these with your small group.

11 What are some stone wall boundaries in your home right now?

12 Are there some rules your children are starting to challenge yet? Share one of them with the group.

13 How do you see the way you speak to your kids as making a difference?

14 How can you avoid using psychological control or damaging words when discipling your child?

15 What is your opinion about spanking your children? Is it a strategy that you plan to use/continue to use?

16 What are some other ways to discipline that you currently use or might start using?

17 Are you planning on making any modifications to how you discipline after reading this chapter?

1. Do you connect with the idea of a tension between how much responsibility you have as a parent to pass on faith to your children and how much responsibility is on God? Where do you fall on that continuum? (One side being it's all your responsibility and the other being it's all on God)

2. What are the pros and cons of either side of that continuum?

3. Where do you think children's primary faith education occurs?

4. What's the danger in thinking it occurs somewhere else?

5. What are you currently doing to support your own faith journey?

6 How would your children see your faith displayed?

7 Do you currently do any spiritual disciplines as a family? Do you see any listed that you might want to start?

8 What are one or two things you can do to encourage faith to develop in your children?

9 How would you describe the "moral therapeutic deism" worldview? What's the problem with this way of thinking?

10 What are you currently seeing in the faith development of your children? Where do you think they are at?

11 Has anything changed in your thinking after reading this chapter?

1 What is your experience with mental illness either personally or with friends and family?

2 Are you seeing any mental health concerns with your children currently?

3 What are one or two things you can do to support your own and your children's mental health?

4 Using the Body, Mind, and Soul framework, how can you lead your family to take care of themselves in each of these categories?

5 What has changed in your thinking after reading this chapter? Is there anything you plan to do differently?

1. How do you and your family deal with the tension to be "in but not of the world"? What does that look like for your family?

2. Is your temptation to be a separatist or a conformist?

3. Is there anything about where you are at that you would like to change to model life as a Christian transformist?

4. How do you see these ideas as impacting how you guide your children in their educational and career pursuits?

1 What rules do you have right now for media for your family?

2 What media rules have you put in place for yourself?

3 What form of media are you the most concerned about its impact on your children currently?

4 Can you see a way to teach the 3-question media discernment tool and response (page 220 and 221) to your children? What do you see as the difference between telling and teaching your children regarding media choices?

5 How do you plan to stay updated on current culture?

6 What rules do you have in your family for phone use/screen time?

7 Is there anything you'd like to change about how much and when phones/screens are used in your family?

8 How could you improve as a mentor to your kids in this area?

9 What have you told your children about posting to social media? Is there more to say to them or do you think they have a good understanding of discernment in this area?

1   How do you feel about talking about sex to your children?

2   What conversations have you already had? What more needs to be covered?

3   Themes in this chapter: view of sex, risks, sexting, setting boundaries in dating, parties, grace. Anything stand out to you? What do you want to ensure you include in your talks with your kids regarding sexuality?

4   Are you conflicted about any of these topics yourself and have anything to work through?

5   Are there some things you feel you need to say to your kids but don't know when or how?

6   What do you think could help make it easier? We suggest you start with bringing up one or two of those to get the group's input.

7   What has changed in your thinking after reading this chapter? Is there anything you plan to do differently?

1. What have you done to help protect yourself and your family in this area?

2. How do you see the effects of pornography on our culture?

3. List and/or brainstorm as a group what you want to ensure you communicate to your kids about why you don't want them to view pornography.

4. Have you had any conversations with your children yet about pornography? If so, what went well? If not, do you feel ready to start these conversations? What is one thing you can do to prepare?

5. Do you know if your kids have been exposed to porn yet?

6   What do you do or plan to do to protect your children from exposure/repeated exposure?

7   Have you formed an opinion on your views of masturbation? How do you see having this conversation with your children?

8   Teaching our kids to be aware of their personal triggers in making poor choices could be helpful in many areas of their life, including temptations with porn. Consider what triggers you have seen in your children already and how you could have this conversation with them.

9   What do you see differently because of reading this chapter on pornography?

CHAPTER 13: DATING

1) What was your dating experience like?

2) What do you wish you had done differently when you were dating?

3) What have you already shared with your kids about dating?

4) What concerns do you have with your children dating?

5) What do you want dating to look like for your kids?

6   What do you see as the benefits of being single?

7   What do you see as the benefits of being married?

8   What do you understand about the definition of small d and big D dating?

9   What rules about dating have you established for your children? For example, at what age are they allowed to date?

10   How will you know your kids are ready to date or not ready to date?

11 What "red flags" in dating are you most concerned about? How do you plan to discuss those with your children?

12 Was there anything discussed in this dating chapter that changed your thinking?

13 What are some conversations you now need to have with your kids about dating?

CHAPTER 14: FINANCES & EDUCATION

1. What did you take away from Brett's points about earn more, spend wisely, give more?

2. What are you doing now to prepare your kids for their post high school education and career choices?

3. What jobs do you hope your children do?

4. Is there anything you plan to do differently with the way you manage money after reading this chapter? How will you communicate that to your kids?

1 What's your experience with drugs and alcohol been like either personally or with friends and family?

2 Do you know if your kids or your kids' friends are using any substances currently?

3 Do you know if any of your kids or kids' friends have experienced any negative consequences of substance use yet?

4 Do you see any of the risk factors listed on page 411 in your children?

5 What could you do to give more socializing experiences to your children?

6 Are you surprised by any of the statistics or stories mentioned?

7 Do you feel better informed after reading this chapter? What's one thing you didn't know before?

8 Have you had any conversations about this topic with your kids yet? What was talked about and how do you think it went? What needs to be talked about next or again?

9 What's one thing you can do to substance-proof your home? (You can refer to the list starting at the bottom of page 435)

10 Are there any next steps for you?

1. Discuss your responses to the Loneliness Survey on page 451.

2. What's one way you plan to strengthen your relationships this week?

3. What's one thing you could do to support friend and family relationships for your children?

4. What's one way you can support someone outside of your immediate family who might be lonely?

5. Has this loneliness chapter changed your thinking in any way? If so, share how.

6 What do you plan to do differently?

This is the end of the Parenting Navigating Everything book study guide.

Thank you for investing your time by contemplating its content through reading, application, and discussion. It is our hope that you have moved towards being a healthier version of yourself as well as deepening your relationship with your children and being better equipped to parent them. We would love for you to tell others about this book and to pray for and support this work. Please consider inviting Brett Ullman to come speak in person to your church, camp, school, or organization. It's been a pleasure walking alongside you these past weeks. May you and your children be blessed.

Website: www.brettullman.com

Social Media: You can find all of Brett's social media linked directly at the top of his website. They are also linked below.

YouTube - https://www.youtube.com/brettu

Instagram - https://www.instagram.com/brettullman/

Twitter - https://twitter.com/brettullman

Facebook - https://www.facebook.com/brettullman11

All the books Brett promotes on all of the topics he speaks on can be found on the Amazon link below. All books are divided up by category so you can find them easily.

Canada - https://www.amazon.ca/shop/brettullman

U.S. - https://www.amazon.com/shop/brettullman